Hello, Family Members,

Learning to read is one of the most important accomplishments of early childhood. **Hello Reader!** books are designed to help children become skilled readers who like to read. Beginning readers learn to read by remembering frequently used words like "the," "is," and "and"; by using phonics skills to decode new words; and by interpreting picture and text clues. These books provide both the stories children enjoy and the structure they need to read fluently and independently. Here are suggestions for helping your child *before*, *during*, and *after* reading:

Before

- Look at the cover and pictures and have your child predict what the story is about.
- Read the story to your child.
- Encourage your child to chime in with familiar words and phrases.
- Echo read with your child by reading a line first and having your child read it after you do.

During

- Have your child think about a word he or she does not recognize right away. Provide hints such as "Let's see if we know the sounds" and "Have we read other words like this one?"
- Encourage your child to use phonics skills to sound out new words.
- Provide the word for your child when more assistance is needed so that he or she does not struggle and the experience of reading with you is a positive one.
- Encourage your child to have fun by reading with a lot of expression . . . like an actor!

After

- Have your child keep lists of interesting and favorite words.
- Encourage your child to read the books over and over again. Have him or her read to brothers, sisters, grandparents, and even teddy bears. Repeated readings develop confidence in young readers.
- Talk about the stories. Ask and answer questions. Share ideas about the funniest and most interesting characters and events in the stories.

I do hope that you and your child er

–Francie Alexander
Reading Specialist,
Scholastic's Learning

D0956837

To Rocky

— *L.J.H.*

To the Cross Country Clan skiers

— *J.W.*

No part of this publication may be reproduced, or stored in a retrieval system, or transmitted in any form or by any means, electronic, mechanical, photocopying, recording, or otherwise, without written permission of the publisher. For information regarding permission, write to Scholastic Inc., Attention: Permissions Department, 555 Broadway, New York, NY 10012.

ISBN: 0-439-20543-3

Library of Congress Cataloging-in-Publication Data available
Hopping, Lorraine Jean.
    Wild earth : avalanche! / by Lorraine Jean Hopping ; illustrated by Jody
Wheeler.
        p.   cm.—(Hello reader! Science—Level 4)
    ISBN 0-439-20543-3 (pbk)
    1. Avalanches—Juvenile literature. [1. Avalanches.] I. Title: Avalanche.
II. Wheeler, Jody, ill. III. Title IV. Series.

QC929.A8 H67 2000
551/57'848—dc21
                                                          00-036573

10 9 8 7 6 5 4 3 2   02 03 04

Printed in the U.S.A.   24
First printing, December 2000

Avalanche!

by Lorraine Jean Hopping
Illustrated by Jody Wheeler

Hello Reader! Science — Level 4

SCHOLASTIC INC.
New York   Toronto   London   Auckland   Sydney
Mexico City   New Delhi   Hong Kong

Chapter 1

Run!

The storm began on a Friday.

For three days, dark clouds
dropped nearly two feet of snow
on Glenwood, Minnesota.
Wind whipped the snow into
drifts that buried parked cars.

Cody and Jesse Pahan [PAY-on],
ages nine and eleven, looked out
the window and made a wish.

Early Monday morning, their
wish came true.
That day, January 6, 1997, was
named a "Snow Day."
School was closed!

The Pahan brothers joined Brian
Schreck, age 14, and Roger
Thompson, age 12.

The four friends hopped on snowmobiles and zoomed across the fresh, sparkling snow.

They knew just where to go after a snowstorm. The gravel pit!

The gravel pit was a big hole in the ground.

Fresh snow lined the sides and bottom like an unfilled piecrust. A round snowdrift formed the edge of the crust.

The snowdrift was as long as two
football fields and as tall as a man.

"Let's do it!" the boys agreed.

One after the other, they jumped
into the drift.
They slid downhill on their
snowsuits at a scary speed.

What a ride!
The boys climbed to the top of
the pit for another fast slide.
Then another.

"One more ride," they agreed.
"Let's all go at the same time."
Brian, Cody, Jesse, and Roger
stood at the top of the drift.

"Ready, set . . ."
Crack!
Roger and Jesse felt the snow
give way beneath their feet.

"Run!" the boys shouted.
But there was no time to run.

The whole drift broke off and fell, taking the boys with it.

The drift smashed itself to pieces as it tumbled downhill.

Finally, it came to a dead stop at the bottom of the pit.

The three youngest boys were buried under several feet of snow. They could not move their arms, legs, or even their heads.

Brian, the oldest boy, had one arm and his head above the snow.

He heard Cody cry for help, but he saw no sign of his other friends.

He saw nothing but snow.

Brian dug out his body, one
armful of snow at a time.
He knew he could not dig out
the other three boys on his own.
So he drove his snowmobile to
the Pahan house for help.

Help came in minutes.
At the pit, Brian showed rescuers
where to dig for Cody.
The snow was so heavy that it
broke some of their shovels.
But finally, Cody rose from his
dark den of snow.

Ten minutes later, rescuers freed
Roger, who was cold but alive.
Last, they dug for Jesse Pahan.

After 40 minutes under heavy snow, Jesse had run out of air and passed out.

His body temperature was so low that his skin was blue. But he was alive!

All four boys survived the scariest ride of all. They survived an avalanche!

Chapter 2

Downhill Disasters

An avalanche [AV-uh-lanch] is a sudden, downhill slide of snow, ice, rock, or mud.
The Glenwood avalanche was small but almost deadly.

In 1999, a far bigger avalanche fell in Venezuela, South America. Just before Christmas, heavy rains turned a hillside to mush. Tons of mud and rock broke loose and slid over a hillside city, killing thousands of people.

The biggest avalanches fall on the world's biggest mountain peaks.

The deadliest ones fall on big peaks that have lots of people on them.

Avalanches kill more people in the Alps mountains of Europe than anyplace else on earth.

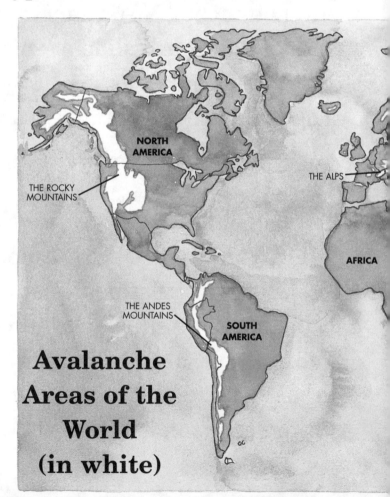

Avalanche Areas of the World (in white)

In 1999, two snowslides met and formed a huge avalanche in the Alps.

Snow tore through towns faster than a speeding train, burying 31 people.

"It was the worst avalanche in 400 years," said one expert.

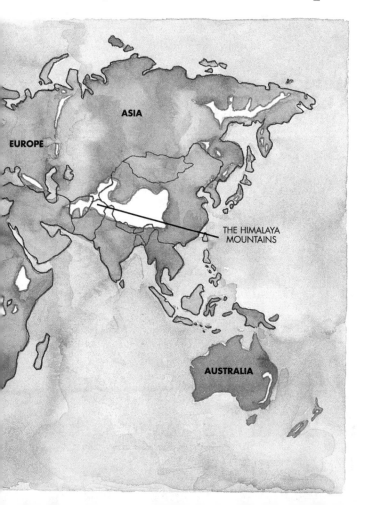

ASIA

EUROPE

THE HIMALAYA MOUNTAINS

AUSTRALIA

Avalanche Deaths in the United States (1985–1999)

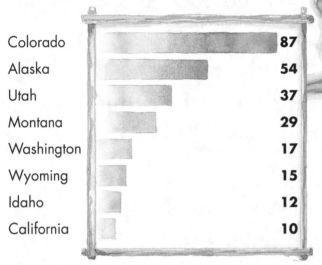

State	Deaths
Colorado	87
Alaska	54
Utah	37
Montana	29
Washington	17
Wyoming	15
Idaho	12
California	10

Source: Colorado Avalanche Information Center

ALASKA

Juneau

WASHINGTON

CALIFORNIA

In North America, most avalanches fall in the Rocky Mountains, a chain of snowy peaks in the West.

By far, most American avalanche victims die in Colorado, a Rocky Mountain state.

Yet the location of the next big killer slide might be Juneau, the capital city of Alaska.

Juneau is surrounded by seven avalanche paths. An avalanche path is a trail where snow often slides.

ROCKY MOUNTAINS

MONTANA

IDAHO

WYOMING

UTAH

COLORADO

21

Avalanche Deaths by Activity

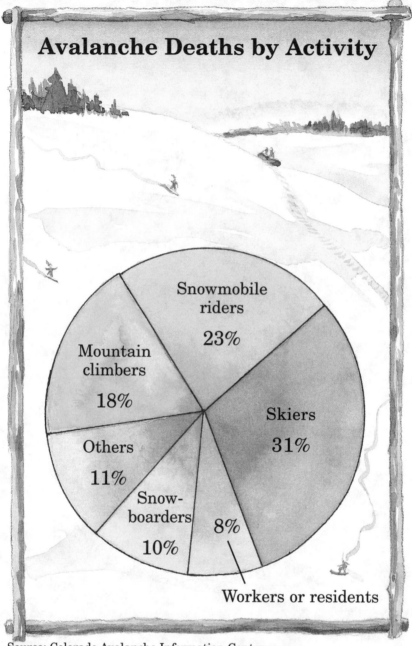

- Snowmobile riders 23%
- Mountain climbers 18%
- Others 11%
- Snowboarders 10%
- Workers or residents 8%
- Skiers 31%

Source: Colorado Avalanche Information Center,
1985–1999 statistics (rounded to nearest whole number)

By far, most people who die in snow avalanches are skiers, mountain climbers, and other winter sports lovers.

Jill Fredston, a snow expert in Alaska, teaches people how to avoid being an avalanche victim.

"Loud noises like gunshots do *not* cause most avalanches," she tells them. "People do."

Skiers and mountain climbers weigh a lot.

Snowmobiles weigh even more.

This weight cracks or loosens the snow, allowing it to tumble downhill.

People cause 19 out of every 20 avalanches that end in death or injury.

Chapter 3

Stick or Slide

Have you ever made a snowball?
Snow tends to stick together.
Snow crystals, tiny bits of snow,
grab one another and hold on.

So what makes snow suddenly
unstick and slide downhill?
What causes snowdrifts to crack
like broken glass?

Why do some avalanches fall
fast and hard enough to snap
trees like toothpicks?

"Understanding what causes avalanches can save your life," says Jill Fredston.

Snow avalanches need three things
in order to happen: deep snow,
gravity, and a slope.

Gravity is always present.
It is a force within the Earth that
pulls objects down, including snow,
mud, rocks, and you.

A slope is land that is slanted. Have you ever sledded or rolled down the slope of a hill?

You fall faster and much easier down a steep slope.

On a very steep slope, loose snow often slides down in little avalanches called sluffs.

The snow cannot pile up deep enough to cause a big avalanche.

"Slab avalanches are far more deadly than sluffs," Jill warns.

In a slab avalanche, a layer of hard snow cracks into slabs, or blocks.

slab avalanche

The giant slabs slide down the slope like rafts down a river.

Slab avalanches usually fall on slopes that are medium-steep.

Those are the very slopes that skiers, snowboarders, and snowmobile riders love.

too flat for snow to slide

so steep that only loose snow slides

just right for slabs to slide

Jill can tell which slabs might
slide by listening to the snow.

As she walks, each step makes
sounds. Crunch. Swish. *Whump!*

A *whump* sound, like a hollow drumbeat, means trouble. It means that a layer of weak snow is lying below a solid slab of snow.

Weak snow is snow that does not stick together. It looks and feels grainy, like sugar or dry sand.

A slab of snow slides on a bed of weak snow like a mattress on a floor full of marbles.

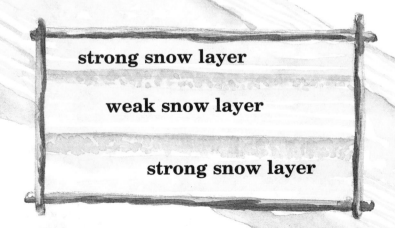

strong snow layer

weak snow layer

strong snow layer

Once, Jill heard a loud snap and felt snow cave in under her feet.

A crack in the snow quickly spread far across the slope. In seconds, a slab snapped off and roared downhill.

crown

starting zone

track or path

slab

It broke into smaller chunks and, finally, into a cloud of powder.

Jill had caused an avalanche! She was not scared, though. She knew better than to walk in the runout zone, a path that an avalanche is likely to follow.

People who do not know better can lose their lives.

runout zone

Chapter 4

Inside an Avalanche

What does it feel like to be trapped in an avalanche? Here is what people have said:

I felt like I was inside a cement mixer, getting all banged up.

I was a rag doll being spun and flipped around, head over heels at weird angles, out of control.

It's like surfing a giant wave . . . then it crashes on top of you.

When the snow finally stops, it is packed so hard it feels like rock.

Imagine trying to find a diamond buried in a mountain.

Finding a person buried under a mountain of snow can be even harder.

In Montana, nine-year-old
Bryant Nutting saw snow bury
his younger brother, Paul, and a
friend, Steve Anders, also nine.
Bryant ran to a nearby school
for help.
The school basketball team and
other rescuers raced to the scene.

But where should they dig?
There was no sign of the boys.
The rescuers cleared away
mounds of snow by hand.
They found Steve, alive.
But they could not find Paul
in time.
He died from lack of air.

In Big Cottonwood Canyon,
Utah, an avalanche buried
Cammy Coyle, age 22.
She could not move.
She could not see.
Nine feet of snow above her
head blocked all sunlight.
Cammy prayed for rescue.

Rescuers jabbed thin, ten-foot
poles deep into the snow.
Seventy-five minutes after the
avalanche fell, a pole finally
tapped Cammy's head.
Most buried victims die within
30 minutes.
Cammy was lucky to survive.

Dogs trained for search-and-rescue
(S.A.R.) often find victims faster
than people with poles.

Jeff Eckland, age 25,
was trapped under five feet of
snow in Kirkwood, California.

A dog named Doc sniffed the
snow for a human scent.

He smelled Jeff and dug him out.
Jeff had a broken back and ribs,
but he was alive.
Like Cammy, he was very lucky.

Most times, S.A.R. dogs do
arrive at an avalanche site in
time to find people alive.

Some mountain-goers carry
a beacon, a radio that beeps.
Rescuers listen for the beeps
to find a buried person.

Poles, S.A.R. dogs, and beacons
help people survive avalanches.
But the best plan is to avoid
avalanches altogether.

Chapter 5

Fighting Back

Teams of workers called ski patrols
study snowy slopes each morning.

They give each slope a color
that tells how dangerous
the area is.

A "red" slope is likely to slide.
A "yellow" slope might slide.
A "green" slope is safe.

Ski patrols have another job.

They look for places where avalanches are about to fall.

Then they make avalanches fall when no one else is around. That way, the slides cannot hurt anyone.

To cause big avalanches, patrols fire powerful guns at slopes up to a mile away.

The heavy shells, like cannonballs, loosen snow so that it falls.

Patrols also explode bombs and dynamite near drifts to make them crack and tumble.

Each winter, Jim Dent,
a scientist, buries himself in
avalanches set off by bombs.
His only protection? A shack.

Snow slides around and over the
top of his wood shack.

Inside, Jim measures the snow's
speed, temperature, and density,
or how tightly packed it is.
These figures show which paths
avalanches are likely to take and
how powerful they are.

People can then choose the safest
spots to build houses and roads.
They can also make buildings
strong enough to stand up to slides.

There is no way to stop
avalanches from falling.
But we can learn enough about
them to stay out of their way.

Avalanche Safety Tips

- Wear a helmet when playing winter sports.
- Stay within roped ski areas or on marked trails.
- Never travel in the woods without an adult.
- Do not step in deep snow on a steep slope.
- If caught in an avalanche, shout to tell people where you are. Then close your mouth to keep out snow.
- Cover your face with your arms.
- If buried, stay calm and breathe slowly to save air.